CLEOPATRA'S NEEDLE

AN ACCOUNT OF THE NEGOTIATIONS LEAD-
ING UP TO ITS GIFT TO THE CITY OF
NEW YORK BY THE KHEDIVE OF
EGYPT, ITS REMOVAL AND ITS
HISTORY AND INSCRIPTIONS
REPRINTED FROM
"EGYPT AND ITS BETRAYAL"

BY
ELBERT E. FARMAN, LL.D.

Formerly United States Consul General at Cairo
Author of "Along the Nile," "Egypt and its Betrayal," etc.

ISBN: 978-1-63923-936-8

All Rights reserved. No part of this book maybe reproduced without written permission from the publishers, except by a reviewer who may quote brief passages in a review to be printed in a newspaper or magazine.

Printed: March 2023

Published and Distributed By:
Lushena Books
607 Country Club Drive, Unit E
Bensenville, IL 60106
www.lushenabks.com

ISBN: 978-1-63923-936-8

PUBLISHERS' NOTE

THE following pages relating to the Obelisk in Central Park, New York City, are reprinted without change from Judge Farman's book "Egypt and its Betrayal," which is an account of the country during the periods of Ismaîl and Tewfik Pashas, and of how England acquired a new empire.

The story of Cleopatra's Needle has been frequently told in magazine and newspaper articles, but the following is the fullest and most authoritative account yet published, and is of such historical value as to warrant its being issued in this separate form.

THE GRAFTON PRESS

CHAPTER XIV

CLEOPATRA'S NEEDLE—NEGOTIATIONS BY WHICH IT WAS SECURED

THE idea of securing an obelisk for the City of New York had its origin in 1877. It grew out of the newspaper reports of the work, then in progress, of transporting an obelisk from Alexandria to London. Paris had such a monument already. London was to have one. Why should not New York, the great city of the New World, be equally favored?

It was erroneously stated in a New York newspaper that his Highness, the Khedive of Egypt, had signified "his willingness to present to the City of New York, upon a proper application, the remaining obelisk of Alexandria." Mr. John Dixon, the contractor who transported to London the obelisk now on the Thames Embankment, was the person, it was claimed, to whom the Khedive had thus expressed himself.[1]

Mr. Henry G. Stebbins, then Commissioner of the Department of Public Parks of the City of New York, undertook to secure the necessary funds for transporting and erecting the obelisk in question. Mr. William H. Vanderbilt was asked to head the subscription, but he generously offered to defray the whole expense of the undertaking. After some telegraphic communica-

---

[1] Mr. Dixon afterwards wrote the writer that the report that the Khedive had had any conversation with him regarding the obelisk of Alexandria or had given him any intimation of an intention of presenting an obelisk to the United States, or to the City of New York, was wholly a mistake; that, in fact nothing whatever of that nature ever took place.

Cleopatra's Needle 143

tions had been exchanged with Mr. Dixon as to the sum that would be required, Mr. Vanderbilt entered into a written contract with Mr. Stebbins to that effect. Only eight days after the first publication of the erroneous statement, Mr. Stebbins addressed to the Department of State at Washington the following letter:—

"New York, 15th October, 1877.
"Hon. Wm. M. Evarts,
   "Secretary of State,
      "Dear Sir:
         "I have the pleasure to enclose two copies of a letter addressed this day to his Highness the Khedive of Egypt, on the subject of the obelisk to which I had the honor of inviting your attention yesterday.
   "Will you kindly send one copy to the Consul-General of the United States at Alexandria with instructions to await the arrival of an authorized representative of Mr. Dixon, mentioned in letter, bringing with him an engrossed copy of the letter, and upon the arrival of that representative, to accompany him into the presence of the Khedive, or in some other proper way to certify to the authority of the letter, and to the authority of the person bearing it.
            "I am, dear Sir,
               "Yours very respectfully,
                  Signed: " HENRY G. STEBBINS."

On the receipt of this letter the Secretary of State, Mr. Evarts, addressed to me the following despatch, enclosing a copy of Mr. Stebbins' letter and a copy of the letter which it was proposed to have delivered to his Highness the Khedive:—

"Department of State,
   "Washington, October 19, 1877.
"No 85.
"E. E. Farman, Esquire, Etc., Etc., Etc.
   "Sir:
      "This department is in receipt of a communication from Mr. Henry G. Stebbins, Commissioner of the Department of Public Parks of the City of New York, relative to the Obelisk which it is understood the Government of the Khedive is willing to present to the City of New York, on due provision being made for its transportation and erection in some public place there. Mr. Stebbins encloses a copy of a letter of which the engrossed original is to be presented to the Khedive by an authorized representative of Mr. Dixon of

London, the engineer in charge of the transportation to England of the obelisk known as Cleopatra's Needle, and solicits the sanction of this Government in the presentation of that letter.

"A copy of the letter of Mr. Stebbins and of its enclosure is herewith transmitted to you. In view of the public object to be subserved you are instructed to use all proper means of furthering the wishes expressed in Mr. Stebbins' letter.

"I am, Sir,
"Your obedient servant,
Signed: "WM. M. EVARTS.

"Enclosures:
"Mr. Stebbins to Mr. Evarts, October 15, 1877, with accompaniment."

Copy of proposed letter of Mr. Stebbins to the Khedive.

"To
"His Highness,
"The Khedive.
"Highness:
"The deep interest excited throughout the civilized world by the removal, under the auspices of your enlightened and liberal Government, of the great obelisk known as 'Cleopatra's Needle,' from Alexandria to England, has been quickened in the United States of America by the intimation conveyed to the people of the City of New York through the estimable Mr. Dixon of London, that your Highness might not be indisposed, upon a proper application to that effect being made, to testify your gracious good will and friendly sentiments towards the American People, by presenting to the City of New York, for erection in one of the great public squares, the companion obelisk which now stands at Alexandria.

"In the hope that such an application may indeed be favorably received by your Highness, an eminent citizen of New York has signified to me his willingness to defray all the necessary costs and charges of bringing this obelisk across the Atlantic Ocean and setting it up in such a situation, there to remain as an eloquent witness alike of the liberal and enlightened spirit in which your Highness administered the affairs of the ancient and illustrious country so happily confided to your sceptre and of your good will towards the youngest of the great nations of the world.

"The generous and public-spirited citizen of whom I speak has requested me in my capacity as a Commissioner, for now many years past, of the Department of Public Parks in the City of New York to lay before your Highness, therefore, through the Honorable, the Secretary of State of the United States of America, this formal application and to say to your Highness that if it shall please you to authorize the removal of the obelisk and its erection here,

I am fully prepared to commission Mr. John Dixon of London at once to undertake the work.

"I am sure your Highness will permit me to say to you, that the successful completion of this work will be gladly and gratefully hailed by the people of New York, and of the United States of America, as a new illustration of the statesmanlike wisdom displayed by your Highness in your patronage of the mighty enterprise which has united the Mediterranean with the Indian seas; and as a new and most interesting bond connecting the Republic of the United States with the Government of your Highness, and with the Egyptian people and Realm.

"I have the honor to be,
"Your Highness's
"Most obedient humble servant,
Signed: "HENRY G. STEBBINS.
"New York,
"Oct. 15, 1877."

I was much surprised by the Secretary's despatch. I had already received information of the publications in New York relative to the obelisk, but was aware that the question was entirely new in Egypt. Soon afterwards I addressed to Mr. Evarts the following despatch and, at the same time, sent him a private letter in which I made other suggestions as to the course that should in my opinion be pursued.

"No. 196.
"Agency and Consulate-General of the United States.
"Cairo, November 24, 1877.
"Honorable William M. Evarts,
"Secretary of State,
"Washington, D. C.
"Sir:
"I have the honor to acknowledge the receipt of your despatch No. 85 enclosing a copy of a letter of Mr. Henry G. Stebbins, Commissioner of the Department of Public Parks in the City of New York, addressed to his Highness, the Khedive, and also a copy of a letter addressed by the same person to you, both relating to the obelisk now standing at Alexandria, which it is desired to obtain and transport to the City of New York.

"On the arrival of Mr. Dixon's Agent, I shall not fail to use, in accordance with your instructions, all proper means of furthering the wishes of Mr. Stebbins.

"I fear, however, that there will be serious opposition to the removal of the obelisk from the City of Alexandria, so much in fact that although the Khedive might personally desire to gratify the wishes of the citizens of New York, he would not think it best to grant their request.

"The obelisk lately removed by the English, having been thrown down many years since, was nearly covered with sand and was not considered of any value to Alexandria. The one now standing, and the monument known as Pompey's Pillar, are the only objects of antiquity remaining in the city that are of sufficient importance to be visited by travelers.

"Should it be impossible to obtain the obelisk at Alexandria, it is not improbable that an application for the one standing at Luxor, or one of those at Karnak would be favorably received.

"The companion of the obelisk removed by the French in 1833, and afterwards erected at Paris in the 'Place de la Concorde,' is within a few rods of the river at Luxor. There are two others at Karnak, two miles below Luxor, and about fifty rods from the river. The removal of one of these might not be impracticable. At least in the case of the failure to procure that at Alexandria, the question might be considered by those in New York, who have taken an interest in the subject.

"I have the honor to be, Sir.
"Your obedient servant
Signed: "E. E. FARMAN."

In the meantime Mr. Dixon had been informed of the steps taken by the parties in New York and of the action of the Department of State. He was much surprised at the manner in which his name had been used. He was directly mentioned in the letter of Mr. Stebbins, which it was proposed should be delivered to the Khedive, as having intimated that his Highness might not be indisposed to present to the City of New York an obelisk. Mr. Dixon, as has been explained above, had never had any conversation with the Khedive upon the subject. He knew enough of diplomatic matters and court usages to understand that it would be entirely out of place for him, a private English citizen, or for his agent, to ask of the Khedive a favor in behalf of the citizens of any country, even his own.

Had the Khedive had any intention or desire to confer a favor upon the people of the United States, he would never have given intimation of the fact to a subject of some other nationality instead of to the accredited representative of our own Government.

Mr. Dixon took immediate measures to inform the parties in New York of their mistake, and, fearing lest I might act on the instructions I had received from the Department of State, he also wrote me the following letter:

"1, Laurence Poultney Hill,
"Cannon Street,
"London E. C., Nov. 16, 1877.
"H. E. The Consul-General of the United States,
"Egypt.
"Sir:
"You will, I believe, have received a communication from Mr. Secretary Evarts requesting you to ascertain from the Government of his Highness, the Khedive, whether he would be disposed to sanction the removal of an obelisk to the United States and present one for such purpose.

"This is all very proper but my name has been mixed up with it as though I were purveyor of obelisks to H. H. ! l I believe it is founded upon a casual remark of mine that if the U. S. wanted an obelisk I thought it possible that one might be obtained. Mr. Vanderbilt offered to defray the expenses.

"You will see whilst a suitable despatch from the United States secretary might have its prayer acceded to, neither my name nor that of anyone else ought to be mentioned.

"I have written to the United States explaining my views and an amended despatch will be sent you. Meantime if you can secure one, well and good, but pray do not mention my name as having suggested it. I shall be glad to co-operate in the novel enterprise, but H. H. has treated me with such consideration that I would not at any price run the risk of offending him as the despatch I allude to would certainly do.

"I have the honor to remain, Sir,
"Your obedient servant,
Signed: "JOHN DIXON."

Mr. Dixon's letter, a copy of which was sent to Mr. Evarts, was received immediately after the sending of my despatch to the latter, on the 24th of November.

I expected soon to receive further instructions; but none came, nor any communication on the subject from any source. On receipt of Mr. Dixon's communication, sent to parties in New York, the whole matter of the obelisk was dropped. After the newspaper publications of October, 1877, which I have mentioned, there was a profound silence. No reference to the subject was made in any of the New York journals for more than a year and a half, and then not until my despatches of May, 1879, to the Department of State giving information of the successful termination of the negotiations which I had personally conducted had been received. Neither Mr. Dixon, nor his agent, nor the engrossed copy of Mr. Stebbins' letter ever came.

During my trip with General Grant in Upper Egypt (of which I have written in "Along the Nile with General Grant"), I examined the obelisk at Luxor, and the two at Karnak, with reference to the feasibility of their removal. My conclusion was that the only obelisk in Egypt that we should be at all likely to obtain was the one at Luxor. No one would think of removing that of Heliopolis, antedating Cleopatra's Needle a thousand years and standing where it was originally placed by Usertesen—a solitary monument marking the site of the once famous city of On.

The larger of the two obelisks at Karnak, the largest obelisk known, in fact, stood where it was placed by the woman-king Hatshepsu thirty-four hundred years before. The smaller one near it, that of Thûtmosis I, whose mummy has since been deposited in the Museum at Cairo, had one corner broken. It was also cracked in a manner that would render its removal without further injury difficult, if not impossible. The only other obelisks then in Egypt, except those broken into fragments, were that of Alexandria and that of Luxor.

I informed General Grant of the correspondence relative to procuring an obelisk and asked his opinion as to the propriety of my attempting to obtain one on my own initiative, as the people in New York seemed to have abandoned the undertaking. He

Obelisk of Ramses II at Luxor; Companion of, but Larger than, That of the Place de la Concorde, Paris.

Cleopatra's Needle 149

replied that he could see no objection to my doing so and advised me to procure one if possible.

On the 4th of March, I had an interview with the Khedive at the Palace of Abdin for the purpose of laying the matter before him. I knew I should not receive a direct refusal. The people of the Orient, especially the better classes, are very polite. They have very little of the brusque, decisive, Anglo-Saxon way of disposing of matters. They seldom give a definite refusal to a request. Courtesy toward a representative of a foreign power would specially require that such a request should be taken into consideration and that a hasty answer should not be given, unless it was a favorable one.

I informed his Highness that the people of the United States desired one of the ancient obelisks of Egypt, and that a wealthy gentleman of New York had offered to defray the expenses of its transportation and of its erection in that city. I mentioned the obelisk of Paris and that of London and the natural desire of our people to also have one in their metropolis. I explained, in the course of the conversation, that our nation was so young and all its works of so recent a date that one of the ancient monuments of Egypt would be much more highly prized in the United States than in England or France. I called attention to the obelisk at Alexandria as the most accessible for shipment, but added that, if his Highness concluded to favor us with such a gift, we should be much pleased with any his Highness might select.

I found the subject entirely new to the Khedive. He seemed, at first, to be surprised at the proposal. However, after various questions and observations, he said that, while it would be a great pleasure for him to be able to accede to my wishes, or to do anything in his power to gratify the people of the United States, the matter would have to be seriously considered. As to the obelisk at Alexandria, he did not think it best even to mention it, since the people of that city would be opposed to its removal.

I did not afterwards make any special mention in the presence of his Highness of the Alexandrian obelisk, although that was the one that was finally given us. As I took leave of the Khedive he said I could call his attention to the subject at some future time.

I immediately sent a despatch to Mr. Evarts informing him of the subject and results of this interview. Other conversations were had with the Khedive regarding the matter, without any definite results. A little later I was present at a dinner given by the Khedive at the Palace of Abdin and it was on this occasion that the first favorable intimation was given in regard to the obelisk. There were from thirty to forty persons present, among them M. Ferdinand de Lesseps. After dinner the company was conversing in groups. The Khedive, who was constantly shifting his place, seemed in better spirits than was usual for him in those sad days of financial embarrassment. He approached me and invited me to be seated. His first words were, "Well, Mr. Farman, you would like an obelisk?"

I replied that we would like one very much. We conversed some minutes on the subject, without his Highness giving the least intimation of his intentions. Some one came to join us and we rose and, soon after, separated.

A few minutes later I was in conversation with M. de Lesseps. This was at the time the Khedive was about to establish a commission of inquiry to ascertain the amount of the net revenues of the country with a view to determining what rate of interest could be paid on the public debt. There had been an almost total failure of the winter crops in a large portion of Upper Egypt, resulting from the unprecedentedly low Nile of the previous year. This rendered it impossible, in the opinion of his Highness, to continue the payment of interest at the rate of seven per cent on the nearly one hundred millions of pounds of Egypt's indebtedness. He had named, or was about to name,

M. de Lesseps president of the commission. During our conversation the Khedive joined us. M. de Lesseps, turning towards him, repeated something I had just said about the best manner of ascertaining the amount of the revenues. Either his Highness did not hear, or, what is more likely, he did not wish to enter upon the discussion of that subject. Interrupting the conversation he said, "Mr. Farman wishes an obelisk."

M. de Lesseps, who was a fine conversationalist, and always polite, agreeable and quick in his replies, immediately said, "That would be an excellent thing for the people of the United States." Then, after a moment's hesitation, during which time the Khedive seemed to await his further reply, he added: "I do not see why we could not give them one. It would not injure us much and it would be a very valuable acquisition for them."

M. de Lesseps had been so long in Egypt that he considered himself as one of the country, and, in speaking of Egyptian matters, was accustomed to say "we," "us," and "ours." The Khedive simply said, "I am considering the matter" and turned to speak with another person who was approaching.

When I made my dinner call, two or three days afterwards, the obelisk was again mentioned. His Highness said that he had concluded to give us one, but not that of Alexandria, and added that he would take measures to obtain the necessary information and inform me of his decision. He at once called his private secretary and directed him to write a note to Brugsch Bey (afterwards Brugsch Pasha), requesting a list and description of all the obelisks remaining in Egypt, and an opinion as to which could best be spared. I thanked his Highness warmly, and, as I was leaving, he said that within a short time his secretary would inform me which obelisk we could have.

It was not many days after this interview that a reception and ball was given at the Palace. Brugsch Bey and myself happened to meet and, after the exchange of a few words, he said in a rather reproachful tone, "I learn you are trying to obtain an obelisk to take to New York."

I replied, "Why not, they have one in Paris, and one in London and the people of New York wish one also."

He answered: "You will create a great amount of feeling; all the savants of Europe will oppose it. The Khedive has asked me to give a description of the obelisks remaining in Egypt, and to state which one can best be spared. I have sent a description of the obelisks, but I shall not designate one to be taken away, for I am totally opposed to the removal of any of them."

Not desiring to enter into any discussion on the subject, I replied in a conciliatory manner, saying that it was of no great importance, that there were a number of obelisks in Egypt, and that the removal of one would not make much difference. He assured me that I would encounter a great deal of antagonism. This was the beginning of an opposition that was to delay for more than a year the completion of the gift which his Highness had deliberately determined upon.

Had this opposition come from Egyptians of position, who would have had a right to be heard, I should have desisted at once, through delicacy, from all further efforts in the matter. It came, however, wholly from Europeans temporarily residing in Egypt, who, whatever might be their opinions and however well founded their conclusions, had no rights to protect against the United States, and, consequently, were not entitled to be considered. It was purely an affair between Egypt and ourselves, and, as no opposition was made on the part of any real Egyptian, I did not feel bound to yield to the opposition of others nor have any scruples about taking every proper means to overcome it.

About this time I was informed by the English Consul-General that the obelisk at Luxor, the only one I then had hopes of obtaining, belonged to his people. He affirmed that it was given

Cleopatra's Needle

to them at the same time that the one at Paris was given to France, and announced that they claimed it and should object to its being removed by anyone else. The Consul-General admitted that he did not know that they should ever take it, but he insisted upon their right to do so. The Khedive afterwards said to me that it was true that the obelisk at Luxor was offered to the English at the same time that its companion was given to the French. They did not take it, but they objected now to its being given to anyone else. Under the circumstances it would not do to interfere with it.

This was a new and unexpected complication. The Luxor obelisk had been offered to the English by Mohammed Ali, fifty years before, because he did not wish to create any ill feelings on account of his gift to France. It was not then accepted and there was no intention of taking it. Another had in the meantime been accepted and removed to London. It was evident that claim was laid to this simply to prevent its going to the United States.

CHAPTER XV

GIFT OF THE OBELISK

WEEKS passed and no note came from the Khedive. In the meantime his private secretary had informed me verbally that no obelisk had been designated to be given to the United States, for the reason that Brugsch Bey had reported no opinion as to the one that could best be spared. I knew that special objections were being made in the case of each obelisk, that all the European influences were combined against me, and that the English claim to the Luxor obelisk was only one of the results of this combination.

Once afterwards, during the spring of 1878, the matter was mentioned by the Khedive. He spoke of the English claiming the Luxor obelisk and said that he had not yet fixed upon one to be given to us, but that he would do so at no very distant day.

Serious difficulties came upon Egypt about this time. The Khedive was harassed and vexed in many ways. M. de Lesseps, well knowing that he could not do justice to Egypt and at the same time please the Paris bankers, had gone to France without entering upon the duties of the Commission of Inquiry. The Commission had been organized, however. It was composed of persons who had been selected in the interests of the bondholders, and its work progressed with rapidity. Among the measures of economy it demanded was the dismissal of many Government employees, and the Americans in the military service of the Khedive were among the first to be discharged. Without any previous notice, they were informed that their terms of service were ended. They all had considerable amounts of arrears of pay due them, and some of them had disputed claims and demands for indemnity which complicated their relations with the Government and rendered a settlement of their accounts difficult.

I was called upon to aid my countrymen and found myself suddenly thrown into an unpleasant contest. In view of this depressed state of Egyptian affairs and the embarrassments with which the Khedive found himself surrounded, there was no time for him to think of the obelisk and any mention of it on my part would have been discourteous. Therefore, I left Egypt about the middle of July, without again referring to the subject, on a leave of absence, with permission to visit the United States.

Early in October, a few days before I sailed from New York on my return, I had an interview with Mr. Evarts in which I informed him of the state of the negotiations relative to an obelisk. He said he would be very much pleased if I could obtain one, and that he was ready to do anything he properly could to aid me.

On my arrival in Egypt in November, I found a great change in Governmental matters. What was called the Anglo-French Ministry had been formed with Nubar Pasha at its head. It had been organized on the theory of "responsibility." A responsible ministry is responsible, while in power, for the government it administers; but it is supposed to be responsible or accountable to some person, or body of persons. This Ministry assumed to act independently of the Khedive, as the English Ministry does of the Queen. But in England there is a parliament to which the Ministers are accountable, to this extent at least, that they must have its support or resign.

In Egypt there was no parliament, all the legislative as well as the executive power being vested in the Khedive. There was a Chamber of Notables, which was sometimes assembled to vote on questions of extraordinary taxation. This Chamber was convoked in December, 1887, or in January following, but was utterly ignored by the Ministry, which even refused to submit to it a report of the proceedings of the Minister of Finance. The Ministers, according to their theory, were independent of all restraint, and, as it afterwards appeared, no one could rightfully remove them. At least this was affirmed.

Such was the Ministry through which the obelisk was now to come if at all, the Khedive, as claimed, having no authority in the premises.

Mariette Bey, who had spent the summer at the Exposition in Paris, had arrived, and I knew he was making strenuous opposition to the gift. He was then at the head of the Department of Antiquities and his opposition could not but embarrass and delay the negotiations. At one time it seemed likely to wholly defeat the intentions of the Khedive.

On my arrival I paid the customary visit to the Khedive and had frequent interviews with him afterwards, but no mention was made of the obelisk for a number of weeks. He finally signified his willingness and desire to complete the gift, but he did not hesitate to intimate to me what I very well knew, that the matter of the obelisk was in the hands of the Ministers.

Though I had little faith in any long continuance of the existing state of things, I took occasion to bring the matter of the obelisk before his Excellency, Nubar Pasha, whom I had never seen until my late arrival in Egypt. He had been in disfavor with the Khedive and had resided in Europe since 1875, being recalled to head the Ministry at the instance of certain European Powers.

I found that he already understood the question, not through the Khedive, but through those who were opposed to the gift. He took a fair view of the matter, however, and said that, if the Khedive had expressed his intention of giving us an obelisk, it

Gift of the Obelisk

should be considered as a "*fait accompli,*" and that there was no reason why the Ministry should oppose it. He promised to see the Khedive, learn exactly what had been done, and then carry out his Highness' wishes. He added, however, that if it were a new and open question, he should oppose it.

Not long afterwards he informed me that he had seen the Khedive, and that his Highness said that he had promised an obelisk and desired to have the promise fulfilled. His Excellency added that he would take the necessary measures for that purpose.

About this time Mariette Bey laid before the Council of Ministers a memorial on the subject, in which he made strenuous opposition to the removal of any of the obelisks of Egypt, and particularly set forth the sacredness of the obelisks at Karnak and Heliopolis. It was this memorial and the declarations of Mariette that afterwards determined which obelisk should be given us. He undoubtedly thought that there would be sufficient opposition from other sources to prevent the removal of the obelisk at Alexandria; that the English would take care of theirs at Luxor; and that, if he could prevent the selection of either of those at Karnak, or the one at Heliopolis, the project would be defeated.[1]

In February Nubar Pasha informed me that the English claimed the obelisk at Luxor and that Mariette Bey was so strongly opposed to the removal of those at Karnak and Heliopolis that he had determined to give us the one at Alexandria, Cleopatra's Needle. He at the same time prepared and handed his clerk a memorandum of a despatch to the Minister of Public

---

[1] Previous to the time of his being employed by the Egyptian Government, Mariette Bey took to Paris the finest collection of antiquities that has ever been removed from Egypt. A large, and the most valuable, part of the collection was obtained only by long and strenuous diplomatic pressure and by keeping the secret, during the negotiations, of what had been found. The collection, numbering about seven thousand objects, is still in the Museum of the Louvre.

Works who represented France in the Ministry, asking him to institute the necessary formalities for its delivery. Whether this despatch was ever sent I do not know. Two or three days afterwards, events happened that threw Egypt into intense excitement and compelled Nubar Pasha to retire from the Ministry.

A large number of Egyptian officers and soldiers had been discharged, without receiving their arrears of pay. It was also just at this time that we were getting the details of the famine in Upper Egypt during the previous months of November and December, and the public feeling had become very hostile towards what was known as the European Ministry. This state of excitement culminated on the 18th of February in a street attack by the discharged officers upon Mr. Rivers Wilson and Nubar Pasha, as they were leaving their departments to go to their noon-day meal. The officers demanded their arrears of salaries and, on payment being refused, took the Ministers back to the Department of Finance and held them prisoners until information was conveyed to the Khedive who came personally to their relief. It was then only with great difficulty, and after some shots had been fired, that order was restored.

Nubar Pasha resigned the next morning. The English and French Ministers, supported by their respective Governments, retained their places and, after thirty days of diplomatic negotiations, the Ministry was reorganized, but under such conditions that the two European Ministers could virtually control the Government. This reorganized Ministry was not destined to last long. Turns of the wheel of fortune were frequent in Egypt and they generally happened when least expected. It is called a country of surprises, and there is an Oriental proverb, according to which only what is intended to be provisional is lasting. An Arab does not finish his house through fear that some accident will befall it or its occupants.

The new régime was supposed to be permanent. Telegraphic

Gift of the Obelisk 159

lines had been freely used and the combined diplomatic wisdom of two great European Powers called into action. Conditions were formulated and imposed that were designed to insure the immovability of the Ministers. When the work was completed, it was supposed that there was at least one unchangeable institution in Egypt. The reorganized Ministry was henceforth to be an immovable fixture in the governmental machinery. But the Arab proverb held good and the structure which rested on laborious negotiations lasting thirty days, endured just eighteen. On the 7th of April occurred what was called the "*coup d'état*" of the Khedive, Ismail Pasha.

The action of the new Ministry was such that the Khedive soon afterwards claimed it to be necessary, for the safety of the country, that he should again take the Government into his own hands and form a Ministry composed wholly of Egyptians. He requested Cherif Pasha to form and take the presidency of a new Ministry. The trust was accepted and the Ministry was formed. Once more the Khedive was the real as well as the nominal chief and head of the Government, but the diplomatic and political circles of Europe were thrown into a state of excitement. At Paris, where the feeling against the Khedive was the most intense, his dethronement was loudly demanded.

I had known Cherif Pasha since the time of my first arrival in Egypt. He was admitted by all parties to be a noble, honest and just man, who never entered into intrigues or speculations. In his youth he had received a good European education. He had commenced his career as an army officer and risen to the rank of colonel, and afterwards had had experience in every department of the Government. Always frank and sincere, he enjoyed more of the confidence of the people than any other person the Khedive could call into his service.

It was not many days before matters were again running smoothly so far as the local Government of Egypt was concerned.

The only difficulties were in Paris and London, where potent influences were at work against his Highness. In Egypt, the native public sentiment was one of hostility to being governed by foreigners. As a result of this sentiment, there arose about this time a faction styling itself the "National Party," having for its motto "Egypt for the Egyptians." It was small in numbers and to a large extent necessarily secret in its action, but its feeling of antagonism to "foreign rule" was in accord with that of the native population.

A number of European Governments were at this time, in consequence of some real or supposed interest, claiming a share in the Government of Egypt, and vying with each other for a preponderance of influence and power. The Government of the United States, having no political purposes to carry out in this country, did not assume the right to interfere with its Government. It was, consequently, able to keep itself free from all political complications. Under these circumstances, there was naturally the kindest feeling among the Egyptians toward our Government and people.

Cherif Pasha was conversant with the negotiations relative to the obelisk. Though the new Ministry had been organized on the same theory of "responsibility" as the one it replaced, I had good reasons to believe that his Excellency would not put any obstacles in the way of the fulfilment of the expressed intentions of the Khedive.

About a month after the so-called "*coup d'état*," political affairs became entirely quiet, and it seemed for the moment as if the European Powers were to acquiesce in the new order of things. A convenient opportunity occurring, I suggested to Cherif Pasha, that I would like to have the matter of the obelisk terminated. He said he would take the first opportunity to talk with the Khedive and that his Highness' wishes, whatever they were, should be carried out. Some days afterwards when I was

Gift of the Obelisk

calling upon him for another purpose he told me that the question of the obelisk had been considered and had been practically decided in my favor, but that he desired to speak to the Khedive once more on the subject. He added that he should see him that evening and if I would call on the morrow at eleven o'clock, he would give me a definite answer. This I was led to understand would be a favorable one. The next day I went to the Ministry at the hour designated, but was informed that Cherif Pasha was at the Palace, and probably with the Khedive.

On my return to the Consulate I stopped to visit the Pasha who held the position of Keeper of the Seal, and who had rooms in one part of the Khedive's residence. I found there two of the princes, brothers of the late Khedive, Tewfik Pasha. We entered into conversation, and coffee was served according to the universal Oriental custom. In a few minutes Cherif Pasha came in, and, after the usual salutations, had a few words with the Keeper of the Seal in their own language. Starting to leave, he gave me an invitation to accompany him, and, bidding good morning to the others, we went out together. On shaking hands with Cherif, I noticed that he was much agitated, and I suspected that there was important and perhaps alarming news from the Cabinets of Paris and London. As soon as we were in the hall, his Excellency commenced a conversation, saying that he presumed I had been to see him, that he regretted not having been at the Ministry, but that he had been detained by important business with the Khedive. We had passed through a long hall and down a stairway and were just going out of a doorway near which both of our carriages were awaiting us when the Pasha said, "It is the obelisk at Alexandria that you prefer, is it not?"

I replied that that one was more conveniently situated for removal than the others.

"Well," said the Pasha, "we have concluded to give it to you."

After thanking him, I said that I ought to have something in writing, confirming the gift, to send to the Secretary of State at Washington. I said further that, though we had always talked of it as a gift to the United States, it was understood that it was to be erected in New York, and that I had been thinking it would be better to give it directly to that city, as otherwise there might be some complication requiring an act of Congress.

Cherif replied, "We give you the obelisk, do as you wish with it." After a moment's reflection he added:—"Write me a note indicating what you wish to have done. State that all the expenses of removal are to be paid by the United States, or by the City of New York if you prefer. Hand the note to my Secretary-general and tell him to prepare an answer confirming the gift, in accordance with the suggestions you give, and to bring it to me for my signature."

Two hours later I handed to the Secretary-general of the Department of Foreign Affairs, at the same time informing him of what the Pasha had said, a letter of which the following is a translation from the French:—

"Agency and Consulate-General of the United States at Cairo, May 17, 1879.
"Excellency;

"Referring to the different conversations that I have had the honor to have with your Excellency in which you have informed me that the Government of his Highness, the Khedive, is disposed to present to the City of New York, to be transported and erected there, the obelisk of Alexandria, I should be pleased if your Excellency would have the kindness to definitely confirm in writing the gift of this monument.

"It is understood that its transportation is to be effected at the expense of certain citizens of the said City of New York.

"I beg to assure your Excellency in advance of the warm thanks of my Government for having thus favorably responded to the representations I have made to the Government of his Highness the Khedive, in accordance with the instructions that I have received on this subject.

"I have every reason to believe that the monument which is thus soon to be transported to and erected in the City of New York, will always be a souvenir and a pledge of the friendship that has ever existed between the Government of the United States and that of his Highness, the Khedive.

The Obelisk, Known as Cleopatra's Needle, as It Stood at Alexandria, Showing the Nearly Effaced Hieroglyphics on the Land Side.

"I beg your Excellency to accept the renewed assurance of my high consideration.

Signed: "E. E. FARMAN.

"To his Excellency Cherîf Pasha, Minister of Foreign Affairs and President of the Council of Ministers."

The next day I received the following reply which I have translated from the French.

"Cairo, May 18th, 1879.
"To Mr. Farman, Agent and Consul-General of the United States.
"Mr. Agent & Consul-General:
"I have taken cognizance of the despatch which you did me the honor of writing on the 17th of the current month of May.

"In reply I hasten to transmit to you the assurance, Mr. Agent & Consul-General, that the Government of the Khedive having taken into consideration your representations and the desire which you have expressed in the name of the Government of the United States of America, consents, in fact, to make a gift to the City of New York of the obelisk known as Cleopatra's Needle, which is at Alexandria on the sea-shore.

"The local authorities will therefore be directed to deliver this obelisk to the representative of the American Government, and to facilitate, in everything that shall depend upon them, the removal of this monument, which according to the terms of your despatch is to be done at the exclusive cost and expense of the City of New York.

"I am happy, Mr. Agent & Consul-General, to have to announce to you this decision, which while giving to the Great City an Egyptian monument, to which is attached as you know, a real archæological interest, will also be, I am as yourself convinced, another souvenir and another pledge of the friendship that has constantly existed between the Government of the United States and that of the Khedive.

"Be pleased to accept, Mr. Agent and Consul-General, the expression of my high consideration.

Signed: "CHERÎF."

It will be seen by these notes that the obelisk was given directly to the City of New York, and not, as is stated in the inscription on a claw of one of the crabs upon which it now rests, to the United States.

On the 22d day of May I sent Mr. Secretary Evarts, the following telegram:—"The Government of the Khedive has given to the City of New York the obelisk at Alexandria, known as Cleopatra's Needle." I also, on the same day, forwarded to him a despatch enclosing copies of the notes that had been exchanged between Cherif Pasha and myself.

The obelisk was secured, but the complications in the affairs of Egypt continued. On the 27th day of June the Khedive abdicated in favor of his son, Mehemet Tewfik Pasha, who, on the same day, was proclaimed Khedive of Egypt.

The experiment of a European Ministry was not tried again. Cherif Pasha was continued at the head of the Administration during the summer, but early in the autumn what was known as the Riaz Ministry was formed.

The final negotiations by which the obelisk was secured had been conducted so quietly that the first public information in Egypt that the gift had been made came from New York through the medium of English newspapers. Very little was then said upon the subject by any of the local journals, but as soon as the Riaz Ministry was organized an attempt was made, through the influence of certain Europeans, to have the action of the late Government reversed. The matter was two or three times considered in the Council of Ministers, and commented upon by the European press of Egypt. The Ministers, however, finding that the gift had been confirmed in writing, by an exchange of official notes, decided that it was too late for them to take any action in the matter. Lieutenant-Commander Gorrings arrived in October, 1879, to effect the removal of the obelisk, and the necessary orders were given to the local authorities of Alexandria for its delivery.

On the receipt of my despatch of the 22d of May informing him of the successful termination of the negotiations, Secretary Evarts wrote me a private letter, and at the same time sent me an official despatch, dated June 13th, 1879. In the latter he said:—

Gift of the Obelisk

"I have to acknowledge the reception of your despatch of the 22nd ultimo, with its enclosures in which you have informed the Department that the negotiations entered into to procure an Egyptian obelisk for the City of New York have been successful, and that the Government of his Highness the Khedive has generously presented to that city the obelisk known as Cleopatra's Needle.

"It is a source of great gratification to this Government, that through the generosity of the Khedive this country is soon to come into the possession of such an interesting monument of antiquity as Cleopatra's Needle. You are therefore instructed to inform his Highness that the great favor he has conferred upon this Republic by making this gift is highly appreciated and that it is felt that such a rare mark of friendship cannot but tend to still further strengthen the amicable relations which have ever subsisted between the two countries and will cause the memory of the Khedive to be long and warmly cherished by the American people.

"The historical account of the obelisks of Egypt, which your despatch contains has been read with interest."

It must not be supposed that the obelisks and other ancient monuments of the country are slightly prized by the educated Egyptians. On the contrary, they are highly valued and guarded with great jealousy. Considering all the circumstances, the Khedive could not have furnished a stronger proof of his respect for the Government and people of the United States than this gift of Cleopatra's Needle. I have abundant evidence of the great admiration he had for our institutions, though he knew that nothing of the kind was possible in the Orient.

The other obelisks that have been removed from Egypt were obtained under circumstances entirely different from those now existing. They were for the most part removed by the Roman conquerors. Only two, besides Cleopatra's Needle, have been taken away in modern times, that of Paris and that of London. The latter was given to England in 1820, at a time when Egypt was in a condition entirely different from that of to-day. Furthermore, this obelisk had been lying for centuries nearly buried in sand and rubbish. It was much injured, and, in comparison with the standing obelisks, little prized. Yet it was considered a gift worthy to be bestowed upon his Majesty, George the Fourth, in return for favors and presents received from him by Mohammed Ali Pasha, then Viceroy of Egypt.

The obelisk now at Paris was given to France ten years later, in 1830, on account, it is claimed, of services rendered to the Government of Egypt. It stood at Luxor, then a small village of mud huts, situated six hundred miles up the Nile and inhabited by a few hundred natives.

There were three other obelisks standing in this vicinity and many colossal ruins, the most magnificent and interesting in the world. The place was at that period, however, seldom visited by Europeans, and the removal of one of its obelisks was not an event to create any opposition. Yet the monument was considered an important embellishment of the city of Paris.

The European press of Egypt, commenting in the fall of 1879 upon the subject of the removal of Egyptian monuments, laid great stress upon the fact that the London and Paris obelisks were both given on account of services and favors rendered by the Governments of the countries to which they were presented, while there was no pretence of any such consideration for the gift of Cleopatra's Needle to the City of New York.

This only proves that the courtesy was prompted by the respect and kindly feelings of a sovereign towards a government and a people who had always been his friends, and who had no selfish designs to further against him, his subjects or his country.

In the acceptance of the obelisk the City of New York assumed

Gift of the Obelisk 167

a solemn obligation toward future generations, towards all of those millions of the citizens of the Republic who shall in the coming centuries visit the great metropolis. That obligation is to preserve the monument which has been placed in its keeping. It has come to us through thirty-five centuries, and, after all the vicissitudes through which it has passed, is still in a fair state of preservation. It would now be a shameful negligence, as reprehensible as wanton destruction, on the part of those having the custody of this noble monument, to allow it to be unnecessarily injured for the want of that provident care which prudence demands should be bestowed upon it.

The injuries it has already received are generally supposed by those who have only slightly examined the subject to have resulted from its having stood for a long time near the sea. This is a mistake. It was not the sides facing the sea that were injured. I have elsewhere shown that these injuries could only have been produced by the alkalies of the soil in which the obelisk probably lay for several centuries, or by fire. It is probable that the principal injuries were caused by the latter agency.

It is well known that polished granite successfully resists all atmospheric influences in cold as well as in warm climates. But when this polish is once removed, and a rough uneven surface is presented, certain atmospheric and climatic influences are injurious.

CHAPTER XVI

THE REMOVAL OF THE OBELISK AND MASONIC EMBLEMS

CLEOPATRA'S NEEDLE is a single shaft of red granite from the quarries of Syene, now Assuân, at the First Cataract of the Nile, seven hundred miles from the Mediterranean. It is sixty-eight feet ten inches in height and seven feet ten inches by eight feet two inches at its base. It tapers gradually upwards to six feet one inch by six feet three inches, terminating in a pyramidion seven feet high. Its weight is about two hundred and twenty tons. It stood upon the sea-shore at Alexandria, fifty feet from the water line, with its base buried in sand and earth that had been accumulating for centuries.

The base of the obelisk, when uncovered, was found to be considerably rounded. It rested on two copper supports cast in the form of sea-crabs and placed under opposite corners. Under a third corner was a stone, but the fourth corner was unsupported. This left a space between the obelisk and its pedestal of eight inches. There was a thin iron wedge wholly oxydized on the top of the stone support. The bodies of the two crabs were about twelve inches long, measuring from the head back, and they were sixteen inches broad and eight inches high. Each, when entire, weighed over five hundred pounds. Bars of the same material as the crabs ran from their upper and lower surfaces into the obelisk and the pedestal. These bars were over three inches square and nine inches long, forming dowels which

Placing the Obelisk in the Hold of the Steamer *Dessong* at Alexandria.

Removal of the Obelisk

held the obelisk securely in its place. The dowels were surrounded and made firm in the mortises with lead.

Originally, there were four crabs, the two missing ones having been removed by the natives for the metal. The remaining crabs were much injured. The claws and legs of one had been removed. The other had only one leg left and even this was broken in turning the obelisk to a horizontal position. It is probable that the crabs were placed under the obelisk as supports at the time of its reërection by the Romans, on account of the rounded condition of its base. One writer conjectures that the form of the crab was chosen to satisfy the superstition of both the Egyptians and Romans.

The obelisk rested upon a pedestal formed of a single block of Syenitic granite tapering upward in about the same proportion as the obelisk. It was seven feet high, averaged nine feet square and weighed forty-eight tons. The substructure on which the pedestal rested was four feet nine inches high and the under surface of its lowest step was only eighteen inches above the level of the sea.

At the time of the erection of the obelisk at Alexandria, a little over nineteen hundred years ago, the surface of the earth at this point was lower than the lowest step of the pedestal. There was a gradual accumulation of sand and gravel to the height of seventeen feet, burying the steps, the pedestal and finally the base of the obelisk. During the same period, there has been a marked change in the relative position of the land and sea. Tombs cut in the rocks overlooking the sea are now partly submerged and constantly washed by the waves. The height of the obelisk, measuring from the base of the lower step, was eighty-one feet two inches.

Lieutenant-Commander Gorrings, U. S. N., was granted a leave of absence to enable him to remove the obelisk to the United States. He was accompanied by Lieutenant Seaton Schroeder, now Captain, and late Governor of Guam, who was a valuable assistant. Heavy constructions were made in the United States to aid in the accomplishment of the work.

When the excavations were finished, the obelisk was encased with planks, and stone piers were erected to support the constructions used in turning it to a horizontal position. These constructions consisted of steel frame-works on two opposite sides of the obelisk, similar in form to the iron piers of a bridge, on the top of which were placed bearings for trunnions. Heavy plates, with trunnions cast upon them, were fastened to the sides of the obelisk by means of long bolts or rods passing from one to the other through their projecting edges. Four pairs of heavy rods ran from the trunnion plates downward and through the ends of heel straps that passed under the obelisk. These straps were double-channeled and fastened to the rods by nuts. When the base of the obelisk was pushed by means of hydraulic jacks from the supports on which it rested, its whole weight was sustained by the rods and, thus supported, it was swung to a horizontal position, turning on its improvised trunnions like a mammoth cannon.

Through an error in the computation of the weight of the upper and lower parts, the trunnions were placed too low, making that part of the obelisk above them heavier than that below. The obelisk, when once started, swung very quickly and struck with great force upon the nest of planks that had been erected to receive it. Happily, it was not broken, though the great throng of people present were startled by the crashing of the planks. It was a fortunate escape from a serious accident to the noble monument. A similar nest of planks was placed under the other end of the obelisk. After the pedestal and foundations had been removed, it was gradually lowered by means of hydraulic jacks to a caisson constructed to receive it.

The caisson was pushed into the sea, towed around the ancient

Removal of the Obelisk 171

island of Pharos and into the harbor. Here, it was placed with the steamer *Dessoug* in a floating dry-dock. The dock was closed, the water pumped from it and the obelisk run into the steamer through a hole made in its side near the bow. The ways on which the obelisk was moved were made of heavy rails of channel iron on which cannon balls were used as rollers. To prevent any injury to the obelisk and cover its uneven surfaces, similar rails of channel iron were placed, inverted, under the obelisk and over the balls. On the arrival of the steamer in New York the same means as those used in Alexandria were employed in unshipping and erecting the obelisk.

The *Dessoug* did not leave Alexandria until the 12th of June, 1880, eight months having been employed in lowering and shipping the obelisk with the aid of the most approved modern appliances which had been previously prepared for this special purpose. Six months more, after its arrival in New York, were required for its unshipment and reërection.

When we compare this work with that accomplished on the banks of the Nile thirty-five hundred years ago, we are unable to find words to express our astonishment at the skill of the ancient Egyptians. The most perfect and beautiful of the existing obelisks is one of those that stand at Karnak. Its weight is nearly twice that of Cleopatra's Needle. According to hieroglyphic inscriptions on its base, this immense monolith was cut from its native bed at Assuân, transported one hundred and forty miles and erected on the pedestal where it now stands, in seven months. The work appears to have been hastened in order that the erection of the obelisk might "commemorate an anniversary of the queen's coronation." We can excuse the satisfaction, the pride, the egotism of the wonderful woman, Queen Hatshepsu, over her marvelous achievement, as expressed in the following inscription which she had chiseled on the pedestal of the obelisk:

"This is what I teach to mortals who shall live in centuries to come, and who shall inquire concerning the monuments I have raised to my father. . . . When I sat in the palace and thought upon him who made me, my heart hastened me to erect to him two obelisks of electrum whose tops should reach the sky before the august gateway between the two great pylons of king Thûtmosis I. . . . When they see my monuments in after years and speak of my great deeds, let them beware of saying 'I know not, I know not why it was determined to cover this monument with gold all over.' It is thus that it hath been done, that my name may remain and live forever. This single block of granite has been cut at the desire of My Majesty between the first of the second month of Pirit of the Vth year and the 30th of the fourth month of Shomû of the VIth year which makes seven months from the day when they began to quarry it."

If we credit the ancient records, there were formerly obelisks of twice the weight of the largest now existing. The broken statue of Ramses II, at Thebes, weighed nearly nine hundred tons. Herodotus mentions a temple of Latona in the sacred enclosure at Buto, Egypt, forty cubits square, "made from one stone" and, for its roof, another stone laid over it, having a cornice four cubits deep.[1] A stone which I saw cut, but still remaining in the quarry, at Baalbec, weighs one thousand tons; and there are in the walls of the temple of that place three stones each weighing nearly one thousand tons. That part of the wall which contains them is of unknown antiquity, but it is probably contemporaneous with some of the great monuments of Egypt, the ruins of which abound with stones of gigantic size.

We know from the ancient drawings and hieroglyphic writings that colossal statues were drawn on sledges and that obelisks were sometimes transported by boat on the Nile or in the canals. By what means the great obelisks were placed on their pedestals

[1] Her. II, 155.

Baalbec, Syria

with the greatest precision, and without in the least marring the sharp edges of their bases, is still left wholly to conjecture.

Obelisks were originally made with a flat base which rested directly on the pedestal. Many of them were thrown down at the time of the Persian invasion and remained on the ground five hundred years, till the Roman conquest. Cleopatra's Needle, originally erected at Heliopolis, was removed to Alexandria in the reign of Augustus Cæsar. Either while lying at Heliopolis or in its removal, the corners of its base were broken off, leaving the lower surface slightly rounded.

The bronze crabs appear to have been placed under its four corners that it might rest more securely on the pedestal. The crabs were discovered in 1877 by excavations made by Mr. Dixon at the time of the removal of the companion of Cleopatra's Needle to London. Copies of inscriptions then found upon the remaining leg of one of the crabs were published by Dr. Neroutsos Bey, an antiquarian of Alexandria, and the crabs and base of the obelisk were recovered with earth.

The inscriptions, as then published and subsequently copied by Lieutenant-Commander Gorrings, inserted by him in his book and inscribed on one of the crabs now under the obelisk, erroneously gave the date of the erection of the obelisk at Alexandria as the year eight of the reign of Augustus Cæsar, 23-22 B. C., instead of the year eighteen, 13-12 B. C. This led to much discussion by antiquarians and historians, both in Europe and America, in consequence of its contradiction of what was supposed to be a well established historical fact, namely, that Barbarus (Publius Rubrius) was not at that time the prefect of Egypt, though he was the prefect ten years later. This fact had been established by a Greek inscription found on the ruins at Philæ, which read, "To the Emperor Cæsar, the August, the Savior and Benefactor, in the 18th year. Under the auspices of Publius Rubrius Barbarus."

174 Egypt and its Betrayal

In 1883, the question was submitted by the authorities of the Metropolitan Museum of Art, where the crab had been deposited, to Columbia College, and by the president of the College to the professor of Greek, Augustus C. Merriam. After a long and exhaustive research, being unable to reconcile the facts of history with the inscriptions as published, the professor had the leg of the crab cleaned of its oxydation. Besides bringing clearly to view some of the Greek and Latin characters that had been supplied in the reading, he found that in the Greek inscription the date was the year IH (18) of the reign of Cæsar, instead of H (8), and in the Latin inscription XVIII instead of VIII.

The correct reading of the inscription is as follows:—

L IH ΚΑΙΣΜΡΣ
ΒΑΡΒΑΡΟΣΑΝΕΘΗΚΕ
ΑΡΧΙΤΕΚΤΟΝΟΥΝΤΟ(Σ)
ΠΟΝΤΙΟΥ

The Latin L represents the word year and is used on nearly all of the dated Egyptian coins of the Greco-Roman period. I alone would be ten, IH, eighteen. The whole inscription may be translated: "In the year eighteen [of the reign] of Cæsar, Barbarus erected [or dedicated] [this monument], Pontius being the architect."

The Latin inscription was on the inner side of the claw and much injured, some of the letters being wholly effaced. The date and the other essential parts, however, were legible. The full inscription, restored, is as follows:

Ψ

ANNO XVIII CÆSARIS
BARBARVS PRÆF
ÆGYPTI POSVIT
ARCHITECTANTE PONTIO

Remaining Part of One of the Bronze Crabs Which Supported the Obelisk, Showing Greek Inscription. The Upper Part Is One of the Dowels.

Professor Merriam was of the opinion that the Greek letter Psi (Ψ) in the upper corner was the initial of the engraver. The inscription may be translated as follows:

"In the year eighteen [of the reign] of Augustus Cæsar, Barbarus, prefect of Egypt, erected [this monument] by the architect Pontius (Pontius being the architect)."

The foundations of the pedestal consisted principally of large blocks of limestone. The whole structure below the pedestal and above the lower surface of the lower step was fastened together with "iron dogs" protected with a covering of lead, in the same manner as iron similarly used is protected at the present day. The iron was of an excellent quality and in a marvelous state of preservation, even where it had been somewhat exposed to atmospheric influences. The entire structure was a magnificent piece of work and showed that the architect, Pontius, would have been entitled, even at this day, to a position in the first rank of his profession.

In this structure were found emblems which have been regarded by many Free Masons as an important discovery relating to the history of their order. Others have taken an entirely different view. The foundations were, with the exception of four pieces, of light-colored gray limestone. On removing the pedestal, there was found under its easterly corner a large block of finely polished Syenitic granite in the form of a cube, except the height was less than the side measurement. I was present at the removal of the first tier of stone. Directly below the granite cube and on the same plane with the lower step, was another piece of granite, the upper part of which was cut in the form of a builder's square. Its long arm was eight feet six inches by one foot seven and a half inches and its short arm four feet three inches by one foot seven and three-fourths inches.

Between the arms of the square was a piece of pure white limestone, four feet long by two wide and nine inches deep. On one side of the square and touching its short arm was an irregular piece of granite, its upper surface very rough, its angles all different, and having, consequently, no two of its sides parallel. On the other side of the stone forming the square was a large block of limestone with its upper surface about four inches below that of the square. It was covered with a thin stone, on the removal of which an iron trowel and a lead plummet were found.

The trowel, which was the shape of a flattened spoon and eight inches long by five wide in its broadest part, was wholly oxydized. The handle was four inches long and three-eighths to one-half of an inch in relief. Spaces had been cut in the limestone block in which these objects had been imbedded in cement. These symbols—the square, the trowel, the plummet, the two granite blocks, the one rough and the other finely finished (the rough and the finished ashler), the white stone and the relative positions in which they were found—are claimed by some members of the Masonic Fraternity to be strong evidence of the existence in the Roman period of an order of Free Masons from which the modern orders have sprung. So many concurrent items of evidence certainly tend to prove that these objects were designedly placed as emblems in the structure. But the presence of all but the trowel and the plummet might be wholly accidental, and these might well be placed by the workmen in so famous a structure as symbols of their occupation without any reference to an organized order.

Alexandria had been a large city for over two centuries. It had recently suffered severely from battles fought within its walls and contained many ruins. These were used as far as practicable in new constructions and probably furnished the material for the foundations of the obelisk. There was nothing unusual in the form of any of the pieces, except that of the square. This stone, when taken out, was found to be twenty-five inches thick, having the part between its two arms cut out and lowered to the depth of nine inches. This space was filled with other stone, including the white block. When it was first discovered, only the upper surface of the form in a square could be seen. The lower part of the stone had the form of a rectangular parallelogram. Taken by itself, the natural inference would have been that it was a part of a large water-basin (from the court of a temple or palace), such as was common in the Greco-Roman period, and that one side and one end had been taken off, by accident or design, leaving the bottom and the other side and end as originally made.

 The inside of the rim of the basin, if it was a basin, had, at its junction with the bottom, three small mouldings or beads and, on the outside at the bottom, the edges instead of having sharp angles were grooved. There was nothing in the appearance of the stone to indicate that it was cut in the form of a builder's square for the purpose of being placed in the obelisk foundation. Its resemblance to a square, when it was in place and the space between the arms was filled, may have suggested to the workmen the idea of adding the trowel and plummet.

CHAPTER XVII

HISTORY OF OBELISK AND INSCRIPTIONS

CLEOPATRA'S NEEDLE comes to us from the golden period of Egypt's history. It was taken from the quarries of Syene, brought down the river six hundred miles, and erected at Heliopolis during the reign of Thûtmosis III, the most brilliant and famous sovereign of the long line of the Pharaohs. The central columns of its inscriptions are devoted to his praise.

Ahmosis, the founder of the eighteenth dynasty, having expelled from Egypt the last of the Hyksos, or "Shepherd Kings," who had ruled the Delta of the Nile for five centuries, led his victorious army as far as Sharuhen, a town near the southern boundary of Palestine which was subsequently allotted to the tribe of Simeon.[1] He afterwards built, to protect his country from further invasions, a series of fortifications on his eastern frontier, not far from the present line of the Suez Canal. He restored peace and order in the interior of his empire and subjugated certain tribes in Nubia that had refused to pay their customary tribute. Contenting himself with the laurels he had won, he turned his attention to the restoration, extension and embellishment of the temples which had been neglected during the long reign of the foreigners.

Thûtmosis I, the second in succession after Ahmosis, was a great warrior and carried his conquests much farther than his predecessor. He led his victorious army through Palestine and

[1] Joshua XIX, 6.

northern Syria to Naharaîm, the "land of the two rivers," which extended from the river Orontes far beyond the Euphrates, and returned to his capital, Thebes, "covered with glory" and "laden with booty." He enriched Egypt by his conquests and by the wealth he afterwards constantly drew from Syria and his southern provinces.

After a short life, he was succeeded by his son Thûtmosis II. Thûtmosis II ruled in the right of Hatshepsu, his half-sister and wife, who was in fact the real sovereign. She was, through her mother, more nearly of purely divine descent than her husband, but it had required a miracle, wrought at her birth, to purify her blood of the taint inherited from one of her maternal ancestors who was not of the royal family.

The kings of Egypt claimed descent from the gods and received homage as divine beings from their subjects. Hence the purity of the royal blood was of the first importance. The king was the "son of Râ." His father was the "son of Râ," and his grandfather and great-grandfather and so back through all his ancestors to the god himself. There were no other earthly families of divine descent with whom to contract marriages. Brothers and sisters intermarried and it was only their children who were of pure royal blood. The male child had the right of succession if he was of the same mother. It sometimes happened that a prince whose mother was only a common woman of the harem succeeded to his father's government, and those whose ancestors were wholly unknown, by success in war or by other means, became *de facto* rulers. These were not regarded by the priests and people as legitimate kings, and they often sought to legitimize their reigns and establish the succession in their children by marrying princesses of the divine blood. They made their wives queens and ruled in their right. The king also often associated with him in his government one of his children, when yet a mere child, because through its mother it was more nearly of the pure royal blood than the father. These means were not always considered sufficient to purify the blood and establish the legitimacy of the reigning family. This could only be done by a miraculous interposition of the ancestral god. Râ, the Sun-god, condescended to become incarnate in the earthly father at the moment of conception and thus the offspring became divine, a "son of Râ." Besides that of Hatshepsu there are two other instances recorded in Egyptian history of the miraculous infusion of the divine essence into the blood of royal families, viz.: that of Amenôthes III, the son of Thûtmosis IV, and of Ptolemy Cæsarion, the son of Julius Cæsar. These inventions of the priests were believed by them to be political necessities.[1]

Thûtmosis I also reigned in the right of his wife. His mother was a mere concubine. To legalize his *de facto* government and continue the divine succession he made Hatshepsu his associate when she was a child.

Thûtmosis II died, after a short and uneventful reign, at the age of thirty. He left one son, Thûtmosis III, whose mother, Isis, was a woman of low birth. He was then a child, but his aunt, Queen Hatshepsu, proclaimed him her successor and continued to rule in his name, as she had previously done in the name of her husband. This nominally dual government continued upwards of sixteen years and ended at a time and in a manner of which the monuments give us no account. It was a prosperous, peaceful reign in which Egypt continued to amass wealth, build and beautify temples and erect other magnificent monuments.

Thûtmosis III was about twenty-five years old when he became sole ruler. He immediately entered upon his glorious career of conquests. About a hundred years had elapsed since the expulsion of the "Shepherd Kings," during which period

---

[1] Maspero's "Struggle of the Nations," M. L. McClure's translation, demy quarto ed., pp. 236, 237.

the foundations of the empire had been firmly laid. But it was left to this ruler, to whom we are indebted for our obelisk, to raise Egypt to the highest rank among the then existing nations. Including the time he was associated with Hatshepsu, he reigned nearly fifty-five years.

His whole reign was a succession of victorious campaigns, which extended the boundaries of the empire and brought to Egypt a constant flow of gold, silver, horses, cattle, sheep and other useful animals, and all the forms of personal wealth known to the commerce of that period.

From the twenty-third year of his reign to the fortieth, he conducted against the Asiatic nations fourteen campaigns. He made long marches in strange and hostile countries, crossing rivers, mountains and deserts, taking by siege and storm stronghold after stronghold and, finally, destroying or subjugating every tribe and people who dared to resist the victorious and beloved son of the god Amon. In the language of the hieroglyphics, he extended his boundaries in the south to the remotest lands of inner Africa; in the west, beyond the tribes of the Lybian desert and along the shore of the sea; and, in the east and north, to the land of the "two rivers" and the "four pillars of heaven."

He was acknowledged by his contemporaries to be the conqueror and ruler of the world and was regarded by his faithful subjects with reverence and awe as a divine being. Under his rule, Egypt became the central point of the world's influence both in commerce and war. His long reign and the immense resources at his disposal, arising from the annual tributes of the conquered countries, enabled him to carry out his early conceived plans for increasing the number and enlarging and decorating the temples of the gods of Egypt, of whom he considered himself an emanation and a part.

It was in this and the immediately succeeding reigns that Egyptian art reached its highest degree of perfection. The centuries that have passed have left us, in most cases, only heaps of ruins; but enough remains to give us a full knowledge of the marvelous monuments of this period. Whether we consider the grandeur of the original conceptions, the grace of the massive forms, the completeness and symmetry of the structures, the elegance and effectiveness of the ornamental designs or the fineness, beauty and fidelity of their execution, we must conclude that the artists of the sixteenth century before our era produced master works that have never since been surpassed. It was Egypt's golden period in power and glory, in war and commerce, in wealth and art, and even historians and poets were not wanting. Indeed, it is to these we are indebted for the very full knowledge we now have of this wonderful people.

Among the monumental works of Thûtmosis III, his obelisks occupy a prominent place. That of St. John Lateran at Rome is one of his, though it appears from its inscriptions to have been finished and erected some time after his death by Thûtmosis IV. It has been somewhat shortened, but it is still one hundred and five feet in height and is the largest existing obelisk, except the unfinished one lying in the quarry at Assuân. It weighs five hundred tons and that of Assuân over seven hundred. It was one of a pair erected in front of the temple of Amon at Karnak. The inscription says: "The king has raised these immense obelisks to him (Amon) in the forecourt of the House of God."

The remaining part of an obelisk now at Constantinople was also his work, and has been attributed to the early part of his sole reign. Like the other Egyptian obelisks, it is of rose-colored Syenitic granite, and its inscriptions were carved in the elegant style of the period. The king here tells us of his Asiatic conquests: "King Thûtmosis III passed through the whole extent of the land of Naharaîm as a victorious conqueror at the head of his army. He placed his boundary at the horn of the world, and at the hinder water-land of Naharaîm."

Cleopatra's Needle and its companion now in London were originally erected by him at one of the gates of the Temple of the Sun at Heliopolis, probably toward the end of his life, about fifteen hundred years before Christ. He restored and beautified the then ancient temple and, according to the inscriptions, built a wall around it in the year forty-seven of his reign.

Heliopolis was sometimes called the city of obelisks from the number of these monuments it contained. It had been a city of obelisks for a long period previous to the time of Seti I, and yet this monarch is spoken of on the monuments as "having filled Heliopolis with obelisks to illumine with their rays the Temple of the Sun." The obelisks, or, at least, their inscriptions, were gilded with gold or other metals. An inscription on the Temple of Amon at Karnak describes certain objects dedicated by the king, Thûtmosis III, to this god. Among them was a "beautiful harp, inlaid with silver and gold, and blue, green and other precious stones," a statue of the king, giving his exact likeness, "such as had never been seen in Egypt since the days of the Sun-god Râ," and "obelisks on which silver, gold, iron and copper were not spared and which shone in their splendor on the surface of the water and filled the land with their light like the stars on the body of the heavenly goddess Nut."

The obelisks stood in pairs at the gates of the temple, to which long avenues, with rows of sphinxes on either side, conducted. Heliopolis was not only one of the oldest cities of Egypt, famous for its monuments and the worship of the bull Mnevis, but for many centuries it was the seat of Egyptian learning. Many Grecian philosophers came to Heliopolis, during its later years, to add to their store of knowledge from the wisdom of its priests.

The long and glorious history of Heliopolis was suddenly ended by the Persian invasion, 525 B.C. From that time, though the priests afterwards restored the worship of the Sun-god, incarnate in the sacred bull Mnevis, the city has remained deserted.

According to Herodotus, Cambyses, the son of Cyrus, when a youth of ten years, promised his mother that when he became a man he would "turn Egypt upside down." The promise was loyally kept. We have no history of the details of the destruction of the sacred city and can only judge of what was done by the cruel and sacrilegious character of the Persians and the condition in which it was afterwards found by Greek and Roman travelers. When Strabo visited it, five hundred years later, 24 B. C., twelve years before the erection of our obelisk in Alexandria, he found only a deserted city, but the faithful priests, tenaciously clinging to the old religion, were still worshipping in the ruined temple. He says:

"Here in Heliopolis, upon a large mound, one sees the Temple of the Sun where the bull Mnevis is kept in a sanctuary. He is regarded as a god, as the Apis is at Memphis. In the front of the mound are lakes fed by the neighboring canal. The city is now wholly deserted. Its ancient temple, built in the Egyptian style, bears numerous marks of the fury and sacrilegious spirit of Cambyses, who ravaged the holy buildings, mutilating them with fire and violence. In this manner he injured the obelisks. Two of these monuments that were not greatly damaged were taken to Rome. There are others of these obelisks, both here and at Thebes, now Diospolis, some standing, much eaten by fire, and others thrown down and lying on the ground."

From this description, the cause of the rounding of the base of Cleopatra's Needle and the injured condition of its sides is evident. It and its companion were probably lying on the ground at Heliopolis from the time of the Persian invasion until they were removed by the Romans to Alexandria. They were not only thrown down and otherwise injured by Cambyses, but they suffered from the alkalies of the soil and the fires of the natives who prepared their food beside them for five hundred years.

The Obelisk, Cleopatra's Needle, in Central Park, New York.

History of the Obelisk

Heliopolis is but an hour's drive from Cairo. The first object seen is its solitary obelisk in the distant fields. There are a few low mounds in the vicinity and occasional ruins protruding from the soil. These and the lone obelisk are the only marks of the site of the once famous city. This obelisk is the oldest of the large obelisks that have been discovered. It was erected by Usertesen I of the twelfth dynasty, nearly a thousand years earlier than the time of Thûtmosis III. Centuries before Abraham was born, even before the recorded time of the flood, the priests of On (Heliopolis) read the deeply cut inscriptions on this obelisk that we read to-day. The same inscription is repeated on each side. The translation is as follows:—

> "The Hor of the Sun,
> The life for those who are born,
> The king of the upper and lower land,
> Khepher-ka-ra.
> The lord of the double crown,
> The life of those who are born,
> The son of the Sun-god Râ,
> Usertesen.
> The friend of the spirit of On,
> Ever living,
> The golden Hor,
> The life of those who are born,
> The good god,
> Kheper-ka-ra,
> Has erected this work,
>
> In the beginning of the thirty years cycle,
> He the dispenser of life forever."

Usertesen was one of the great kings of the twelfth dynasty and had a prosperous reign of forty-five years, including ten years in which he was associated with his father. In the third year of his reign, after counseling with the high officials of his court, he ordered the "raising of worthy buildings to the Sungod Râ." He either restored or enlarged the temple, which was already ancient even in that remote period. When the great gate was finished, he erected at its entrance a pair of obelisks, of which the obelisk now standing was one. Its companion was often mentioned by the old Greek and Arab writers, and remained standing till A. D. 1160, when it fell and was broken.[1] The pyramidions of these obelisks were covered with copper caps, which, according to these writers, were of great weight and value. They also had figures carved upon them.

The New York obelisk, before its removal from the sacred city of Heliopolis, had long outlived its own civilization. It had passed through the whole of Egypt's golden period. It had looked down upon the boy Moses, as he went daily, with the noble youths of the land, to receive instruction from the priests of the Temple of the Sun; and Moses, on his part, beheld with admiration the then golden hieroglyphs, that so long puzzled the wise men of modern times, but which he read as a student reads his Latin. It had beheld the chosen people of God in the days of their oppression and witnessed the excitement at the time of the Exodus—the hurrying to and fro of the priests of the temple and the groups of the people in the public places of the city discussing the great event.

It had afterwards watched for eight centuries the passing of the generations during the reign of the Pharaohs, and had looked down not only upon these monarchs, but upon all the long lines of scholars who came to seek knowledge in this famous city of learning. It had then mutely witnessed the conquest of the

---

[1] De Lancy in his notes accompanying his translation of Abel-ul-Latif, from the Arabic into French, cites at length the statements of these writers relative to this obelisk.

History of the Obelisk

Persians and seen the city of On and its temples destroyed, and itself and many of its companion obelisks become victims of the vengeance of the sacrilegious soldiers of Cambyses.

Afterwards, lying upon the ground, where it had been left by the Persians, it had seen Plato in his daily walks pursuing his study of philosophy and astronomy. It had then beheld the coming of Alexander the Great into its surrounding ruin and desolation and his warm reception by the people as their deliverer from the yoke of the Persians; and later, the three hundred years' reign of the Ptolemies.

On the coming of the Cæsars, it had left the ruin and decay of its inland town and been transferred to the busy seaport of Alexandria. Here, standing upon the seashore, a beacon to mariners for nineteen hundred years, it watched the rolling waves and the coming and going of the ships on the one side and the kaleidoscope of human events on the other.

Rebellions and insurrections, invasions and conquests; the struggles between paganism and Christianity, between Christianity and Mohammedanism and between the different dynasties of Arabs and Turks; the successive reigns of Sultans, Khalifs and Mamelukes; the conquest of Napoleon and the land and sea battles between the English and French were all seen by this ancient monument while standing at Alexandria. What it is to see during the coming centuries, in its new home within a metropolis that had not even an existence when it was three thousand years old, can only be related by historians to be born in the distant future.

The ancient Egyptians had a literature far surpassing that of any other of the early peoples. Only a small part of it has come to us. Many hundreds of inscriptions, however, have been preserved on stone and papyrus. The more they are studied the greater is the admiration of the scholar. Some of these inscriptions are historical; others relate to religious beliefs.

Of all the Egyptian writings, the inscriptions on the obelisks are the least interesting. They are devoted to the boastful self-praises of the kings and the affirmation of their descent from the gods. Those on the pyramidion and the central columns of the New York obelisk were inscribed by Thûtmosis III. Nearly three hundred years later, Ramses II used the vacant space on each side of the central column. He was not only famous for his numerous and great works, but he was also the great appropriator of the works of his predecessors for the record of his own name and fame. The two outer columns which he inscribed on each face of the obelisk tell us of his abundant years, his great victories, and that he is the son of the Sun-god Râ, the issue of his loins.

Four hundred years later, Osarken I placed close to the outer edge of each face, near the base of the obelisk, inscriptions informing succeeding generations that he was the king of Upper and Lower Egypt, and a descendant of the Sun-god. This king, under the Bible name of Zerah, was defeated by Asa in a great battle in the south of Palestine.[1]

On the east face of the pyramidion, Thûtmosis III is represented as a sphinx couchant on a pedestal, holding in his hands two vases and in the act of offering a libation to the hawk-headed Ra-Harmachis, the Sun-god of On (Heliopolis). Thûtmosis is here called, "The Good God," "Lord of the Two Lands" (Upper and Lower Egypt), "Men-Kheper-Ra," and "The Bull of Victory arisen in Thebes, son of the Sun, Thûtmosis." Under the vases in the half-effaced inscription may be read, "Giving Wine."

The central column of hieroglyphs, that of Thûtmosis III, on the east face of the obelisk, is translated as follows:

[1] II Chron. XIV, 9–13.

Banner-name
"The crowned Horus
Bull of Victory
Arisen in Thebes.

. . . .

"The lord of the Vulture and Uræus crowns
Prolonged as to kingdom,
Even as the sun in the heavens.
By Tum lord of On begotten,
Son of his loins, who hath been
fashioned by Thot,
Whom they created in the great-temple
With the perfections of their flesh,
Knowing what he was to perform,
Kingdom prolonged through ages,
King of Upper and Lower Egypt
Men-kheper-ra (Thûtmosis III),
Loving Tum, the great god,
With his cycle of divinities,
Who giveth all life stay and sway,
Like the sun forever."

Central column, north face.

Banner-name
"The crowned Horus
Tall with the southern crown
Loving Ra.

. . . .

"The king of Upper and Lower Egypt,
Men-kheper-ra (Thûtmosis III),
The golden Horus, content with victory,

Who smiteth the rulers of the nations—
Hundreds of thousands;
In as much as father Ra
Hath ordered unto him
Victory against every land,
Gathered together;
The valor of the scimeter
In the palms of his hands
To broaden the bounds of Egypt;
Son of the Sun, Thûtmosis III,
Who giveth all life forever."

INSCRIPTIONS OF RAMSES II

Translation of the south column of the east face.

Banner-name
"The crowned Horus,
  Bull of victory
  Son of Kheper-ra.
        .   .   .   .

"The king of Upper and Lower Egypt
  User-ma-ra (Ramses II).
  The chosen of Ra, the golden Horus
  Rich in years, great in victory,
  Son of the Sun, Ramses II,
  Who came forth from the womb
  To receive the crowns of Ra;
  Fashioned was he to be the sole ruler,
  The lord of the Two Lands,
  User-ma-ra (Ramses II),
  The chosen of Ra, son of the Sun,
  Ramessu Meiamun (Ramses II),

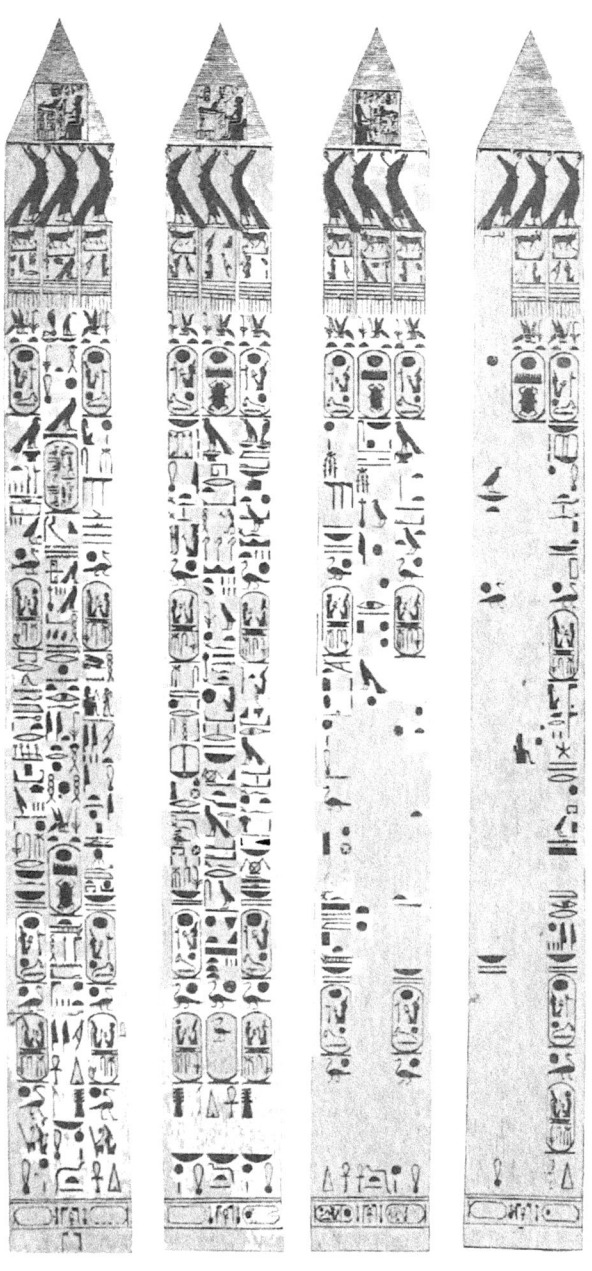

The Hieroglyphics on the Four Sides of the Obelisk in Central Park, New York.

Glorified of Osiris
Like the Sun life-giving forever."

North Column.
Banner-name
"The crowned Horus
Bull of Victory
Loving Ra.

. . . .
"The king of Upper and Lower Egypt
User-ma-ra (Ramses II),
The chosen of Ra,
The Sun born of divinities,
Taking the Two Lands,
Son of the Sun,
Ramessu Meiamun (Ramses II);
The youth
Beautiful for love,
Like the orb of the Sun
When he shines in the horizon,
The lord of the Two Lands,
User-ma-ra (Ramses II),
The chosen of Ra,
Son of the Sun
Ramessu Meiamun,
Glorified of Osiris,
Life giving like the Sun forever."

There are also some nearly effaced hieroglyphics at the bottom of the obelisk. They have been translated as: "Life gracious-god, Ramses II." This phrase is repeated several times at the bottom of each face.

The other inscriptions on the different sides of the obelisk are of the same character and to a large extent repetitions of those of which the translations have been given.

On two sides of the pyramidion, Ramses III, as a sphinx couchant, is represented as offering libations to the Sun-god, Ra-Harmachis (the rising sun) and on the other two sides to Tum (the setting sun).

www.ingramcontent.com/pod-product-compliance
Lightning Source LLC
Chambersburg PA
CBHW040311050426
42450CB00019B/3459